Zipper

AND FRIENDS

Lloyd J. Goddard

All graphics and clip-art images are from Public Domain sources.

Published by Sunroom Publishing
https://www.sunroompublishing.com
Copyright © 2015 Lloyd J. Goddard
All rights reserved.

Printed in The United States of America

ISBN-13: 978-0692447451
ISBN-10: 0692447458

DEDICATION

To my wife, Martha

In Memory of

Josie Blackwell

Contents

ACKNOWLEDGMENTS.. vii

I'M ZIPPER! 1

ZIPPER'S CLOSE CALL 5

ZIPPER MEETS SKIPPY 9

A NEW FRIEND 13

A RAINY DAY 17

LUNCH WITH HOWARD.. 21

ZIPPER MEETS ANGIE 23

A GOOD NEIGHBOR.. 25

THE BLESSED EVENT.. 29

ZIPPER'S DATE 33

ZIPPER GETS A SHOCK.. 37

THE WEDDING PLANS... 41

WEDDING DAY 45

CAST OF CHARACTERS

ZIPPER --------------------------------THE STAR SQUIRREL

CLANCY------------------------------ZIPPER'S FRIEND

HARRY ------------------------------CLANCY'S FATHER

FIFI ----------------------------- CLANCY'S SISTER

HENRY-----------------------------THE MEAN OLD DOG

THOMAS ------------------------- THE MEAN TOM CAT

SKIPPY ----------------------------THE PUPPY

HOWARD ------------------------THE RACCOON

WOODY ---------------------------THE WOODPECKER

ANGIE----------------------------MAMA WOODPECKER

HOOTIE OWL---------------------VILLAGE ELDER

ACKNOWLEDGMENTS

TO:

John, Angela, Alexandria, and Madison Schumaker.

Dennis and Twana Meade.

David and Jamie Meade.

Hunter and Rebecca Meade.

Gary, Teresa, Josh, Jake, and Jonah Blackwell.

Elby Blackwell and Shirley Stansbury.

For all the inspiration, faith and love extended to me

when I needed it most.

1

I'M ZIPPER!

Hello there, my name is Zipper. I am very happy to meet you. I am a one year old squirrel, you've probably seen me in the trees around your home or running back and forth along the power lines high above. My fur is like angel hair, a little gray mixed with brown. My tail is long and fluffy with a cute curl and helps me to balance when I do my high wire acts.

My home is a great Maple tree on the corner lot where the Bensons live. That's probably where I was born, and the only home I have ever known. The tree is hollow about half way up and has a hole in it made by a woodpecker some time ago. That's my home, nice and cozy with plenty of room to store nuts and things for winter. Sometimes a bird will stop in looking for a place to live, and I tell him "*Sorry bud, no vacancy.*" It's quite comfortable now being padded with straw, feathers, etc. that I've gathered from the surroundings.

There are lots of others around that have become my friends. There's Woodrow the red headed woodpecker who's known as the village carpenter since he is always busy, but very noisy making new homes in the tree trunks. He is most likely nuts from all the head banging required by his job. At times I may refer to him as Walnuthead.

Then there's Harry, he is a lot like me except that he has more gray than me, maybe because he's a lot older. He occasionally comes by to visit and always wants to stay for a meal. I think maybe he has a harder time finding food because of his age. Harry has a son, Clancy, and a daughter, Fifi, running around the neighborhood. He told me of another of his sons that he lost when it was run over by the

Bensons teenage daughter learning to drive. Harrys mate Cindy, passed away several years ago.

Fifi is about my age and very pretty. I don't get to see her very often, I suppose she keeps busy cleaning house and never comes outside to scavenge for food.

The neighborhood has no shortage of evil doers. There's a mean old dog, Henry, that belongs to the Bensons. He is quite old which is the saving grace for me and my friends. Henry is slow and not too agile making him easy to escape from.

They also have a cat named Thomas. He's a big, fast, very agile, and ferocious Tom cat. Once he gets you in his sights, you had better be fast and a good tree climber. He's also good at tree climbing and has a long arm with big claws that can reach back into the woodpecker hole, almost to the back.

Now that you know me, come along as my friend and see things from a different point of view.

ZIPPER

2

ZIPPER'S CLOSE CALL

It was late spring now, almost summer. The perfect time to start stocking up the pantry for winter. There's not much competition finding food since Henry and Thomas have been in charge of population control. There are several Oak trees and a Pecan tree or two nearby which makes it pretty easy to stock up. Acorns are my favorite because it's easy to get a good bite on them to crack their shell. Pecans on the other hand, are more tasty, but harder to open.

What a fine day it is, the Sun is warm with very little wind. A good day for high wire walking. Clancy and I usually worked together so that one could gather nuts while the other stood watch high above. When I was gathering and

Thomas or Henry was spotted, Clancy would begin to bark wildly which in English means, *"Run for your life."*

Here I am happily gathering acorns. I had both cheeks crammed full and was about ready to return home and give Clancy a chance to gather. All of a sudden Clancy began to bark like crazy and when I turned to look around, there was Thomas almost on top of me.

He was hunkered down ready to pounce on me. My fur stood straight up and my tail fluffed up about twice its usual size. Luckily I was only a few feet from the trunk of the tree and was able to reach it in one leap. Thomas was right on my heels, however, I was a little better climber than he was and when he got too close I moved to the other side of the tree. He didn't know it until he had passed me by. That gave me time to come down and head for the power pole and do my high wire act.

Thomas was good at walking a fence, but no match for me on a wire. I had narrowly escaped doom that day, thanks to Clancy.

CLANCY

FIFI

3

ZIPPER MEETS SKIPPY

Every day was not a work day for us, some days were reserved just for fun and this was such a day. The restocking for winter was coming along nicely, so we decided to do some exploring in the neighborhood. Just down the street we ran into a wee pup. At first we thought, "*Oh no, not another chaser*"! The little pup ran up to us, his tail wagging, sniffed our noses and said, "*My name is Skippy, what's yours?*"

We were both in shock that we had not been pounced on immediately. With a small gasp we told him our names and Clancy muttered, "*You're a funny looking squirrel.*" Then Skippy answered, "*But I'm not a squirrel, I'm a dog and you* sure are *funny looking dogs*." It took a few minutes for them to get this mix up sorted out and they decided they were destined to be friends.

Skippy didn't live far away, he always stayed inside at night and was let out each morning to romp and play. He said he had lots of toys, but would rather run around looking for adventure. He appeared to be healthy and well cared for. That probably accounted for his good nature.

I said to Skippy, "Come *with us, we're going to play tag on the high wires*." Skippy replied, " *I can't do that, I can't climb*." Then Clancy blurted out, " *You mean you can't climb up a tree or anything?*" With a sad look on his face Skippy asked, "*Does that mean I can't be friends with you?*" I said "*Oh no, it just means that we will have to play on the ground, but it's a lot more fun on the wires. We have to be very watchful for Henry and Thomas, they will catch us if they can*."

As the day wore on we played and made up new games that all three of us could play together. Skippy showed us all of his toys which consisted of a little rubber ball and a couple of bones. We loved the ball, but couldn't quite understand what the bones were for. Nevertheless, a good time was had by all and it was a very good day.

ANGIE

SKIPPY

4

A NEW FRIEND

One day as Clancy, Skippy and I were playing and scouting the area for new adventures when it began to rain. Skippy said, *"Oh my! let's run under this old shed and not get wet."* They managed to get through a small hole in the wall where the boards had rotted away.

Once inside where it was nice and dry, they discovered they weren't able to see. It was very dark and they began to get a little scared. As they huddled together to get warm, Skippy said, *"Look, look, what on earth is that?"* As they all slowly got accustomed to the dark, they could see something. It was two shining objects that blinked and moved around. *"What ever could it be, "* said Clancy. I replied, *"I don't know, but I think I would rather be out in the rain"*. All at once all three of us tried to get through the hole at the same time until finally we all got out. When we felt safe, we looked back at the old shed and saw the oddest thing we had ever seen come out into the light.

It had a pointed face with two big eyes and a very long tail for its size. Skippy began to bark at it because he was afraid. About then it began to speak, *"Please don't hurt me, I was afraid and only trying to keep dry."* Skippy said, *"You were afraid? You scared us because we had never seen eyes that shined in the dark. My name is Skippy and these are my friends, Clancy and Zipper. What is your name?"* The Raccoon said, *"My name is Howard, I am a Raccoon and I don't know where I live. I was playing and wandered off, now I don't know where I am".*

Clancy said *" You can come with us if you like and we will help you find your home."* Howard *said, "That would be* great." So we all went off together in search of Howard's home.

I asked Howard, "Can you remember anything about your home?" Howard said, "All I know is that it was dark inside all the time and water would come through when it rained",. Then Skippy replied, "That sounds like the thing that is back where Henry lives, you know, it goes under the street." And I said, "Yes, that does sound like it may be the place, let's all go and see!" So we all went back to the Bensons house on the corner and sure enough, it was Howard's home. "Oh, thank you all so much, I could never have found it by myself", said Howard. Clancy said, "Now that we know where you live, let's all go and have some fun".

With that, we all wandered off to explore new and exciting things being ever so watchful of cars that could squash you flat, also keeping an eye out for Henry and Thomas

HENRY

5

A RAINY DAY

Well, looks like this rain will last all day. I may as well go to visit with Harry for a spell, I'm sure he would enjoy seeing someone besides Clancy for a change. I brushed my teeth, combed my fur, and fluffed my tail and I was ready to go, after all, a pretty girl lived there too. Once I arrived at Harry's, I found Clancy asleep as usual and Fifi busy cleaning. Picking up after Harry and Clancy was a full time job.

I like to play chess, but there's no one around that knows how to play, so I had to settle for checkers with Harry. Now Harry was from the "old school" and he new the game of checkers inside and out. I have played with him many times, always losing. There have been times when I thought I had him beat for sure, then he would make a move that he had been planning ahead and wipe me out. Nevertheless, I enjoyed our time together. He usually told me of times when he was a kid and his many adventures. Harry was raised in the forest where he knew many friends and there was a new adventure behind every tree. Of course the forest also had its share of evil doers who always wanted to invite you to dinner.

"Why do you always do that Harry? Every time I get ready to king my man you somehow manage to jump him and I have to start all over again. Boy! I wish my grandpa was here, he would show you a thing or two!" I said. Harry would let me win once in a while so I wouldn't get bored.

Harry must have awakened Clancy with all his chuckles and he said,"Let's go outside and visit with Howard for a while. We'll be out of the rain there and maybe we can meet his family." I agreed and thanked Harry for his patience with me. We found Howard hunkered down in his drain pipe trying to keep warm. Much to our surprise, Howard was alone. I asked him,"*Where are your parents? We were hoping to meet them.*" Howard replied, "*I don't know, I hardly knew them when they disappeared. They went out for food one night and never came back.*" Clancy said, "*Aren't you afraid all alone?*" Howard answered, "*Sometimes, but then I hardly ever have any intruders except maybe a frog or two.*" We felt sorry for Howard and didn't mind staying with him a while. The rain soon stopped and Howard said, "*I know where we can find all the food we can eat and if you want I will take you there now.*" We agreed and went with him.

HOWARD

6

LUNCH WITH HOWARD

Howard led us down the street to an old house with a fence all around. He had found a gap in the fence big enough for all of us to get through. The only thing he didn't tell us was that a very nice lady lived there with a bunch of cats. That didn't bother Howard because they never bothered him, they would just sit back and watch him eat all the while wondering what he was.

When we rounded the corner and saw a yard full of cats, we froze in our tracks. Howard said, *"Come on, they won't hurt you."* Not trusting his judgement Clancy said, *"You go first Zipper, if you don't get eaten alive, I'll come later."* I looked around and sure enough there were paper plates lying all around with food in them just sitting there for anyone. Apparently all the cats had eaten their fill and just wanted to lay around and nap. I slowly approached the food with my eyes firmly affixed on the cats, but to my surprise, they paid no attention to me.

As I let out a sigh of relief I said to Clancy, " *Come on over, this is great!*" Clancy hesitated for a minute or two and finally crept over and began to eat. This was surely paradise, I thought, you don't even have to break shells or anything. After we ate, we went back through the fence and said good-bye to Howard; it was getting dark and time to go home.

7

ZIPPER MEETS ANGIE

"Good gosh! What is that racket?" I yelled, as I jumped straight up in the bed. I looked outside to discover Walnuthead pecking on my tree not two feet away just above me. I said, *"What on earth are you up to Woody?"* Woody replied,*"I've got to make a home for my sister, Angie, her home is being cut down tomorrow and she will be homeless if I don't hurry."*

Now this is really upsetting. The one thing I don't need is another walnut head in the neighborhood. He said, *"She is ready to start a family and cannot be left outside."* After hearing that, I thought I should help in any way I can and at least try to be a good neighbor. Walnuthead worked feverishly all day without even stopping to eat. Surely his head must be throbbing by now.

Woody finally finished his work just before dark and I convinced Clancy to help me gather the materials Angie would need for her nest. After a couple of hours we had gathered enough to provide her with a very nice and comfortable bed.

The next morning bright and early Angie appeared along with Woody to survey her new home. She was really surprised to see all the work we had done to make her a nice home. I felt very good knowing that I had helped. Angie thanked us with tears in her eyes and shrouded us with her wings. Woody had scavenged something for her to eat and she settled into her new home. I felt so proud.

Feeling all warm inside, I gathered up Clancy, Skippy, and Howard, then went out to look for new adventures.

8

A GOOD NEIGHBOR

Now that I have a new neighbor I must learn to get along with her, something new to me, never having a neighbor before. It's been almost two weeks since she moved in and Woody tells me that she has three eggs now. She won't be free to leave her nest now to look for food, so Clancy and I decided to provide her with as much as we could. We will try to give her some of the shelled out pecans that we have stockpiled, after all, they are tasty for us and she may like them as well.

While I'm thinking about food, I think I'll find Howard and see if we can go for a picnic of cat food like we did before. I really wish some of those cats could be friends with us. We could have lots of fun in the trees. I don't think my new neighbor would like it very much since Angie will have little ones pretty soon, so it might be wise to hold off on cat friends for a while.

When we arrived at the home of all the cats we discovered there was very little food left for us. We ate what there was and began to look around for scraps when all of a sudden the lady that lived there opened her door. That startled us and we started to run away, when we heard her calling to us. We turned to look and lo and behold, she was putting out more food just for us. We stopped in wonder thinking why on earth did she do that! After she went back inside Howard said, "*Hold on for a minute and if she doesn't come back out we'll go over and help ourselves.*" As it turned out she was just being kind and we enjoyed it.

With full tummies now, we went down the street to meet up with Skippy. Skippy had been to the doctor for a checkup and a bath. Howard *said, "I don't think I would like* a bath very much. I hate getting wet when it rains." Clancy said, "Me too, I don't like it either, but when you get caught out in the rain you don't have much choice." Skippy did look nice though, with fluffy fur and a kerchief around his neck. It gave him sort of a western look.

Down the street a new house was being built and it was going to be very big, bigger than the Bensons even. Clancy said, "Boy!, this will be a swell place to play when the workmen leave today." Skippy said, "Yes, "but we'll have to get home before it gets dark." We spent the rest of the day watching the men work, waiting for them to leave so we could play.

9

THE BLESSED EVENT

It's been a while that Angie started sitting on her eggs and Clancy and I have been busy keeping her supplied with food. Woody also came by with some of her favorite snacks, all in all, she has remained quite healthy. One afternoon I heard Angie singing at the top of her voice for all the neighborhood to hear. She was singing,"*Oh joy, oh joy, it's happening, it's happening!*" I ran to her place to see what she meant. I said, " *Angie, what are you so excited about?*" She replied, "*They're hatching, the eggs, they're hatching!*" I said, "*Oh my, I'd better tell the others, we have to celebrate.*"

Woody, Clancy, Fifi, Harry, and I sat patiently by and watched as each egg hatched. The babies were funny looking with no feathers and big eyes. In my opinion they were downright ugly, but to Angie they were beautiful and she was very happy indeed! Poor Woody was exhausted, having paced the floor for the whole time the event was taking place since her mate had not returned from his trip South. He said, *"I must go quickly to find food for the little ones. They can't eat nuts and things like we do, I must hurry, I must hurry."*

All this time I was sitting next to Fifi and as she witnessed the event she occasionally looked over at me long enough to make eye contact. *"Boy, is she pretty,"* I thought. As the evening wore on, Fifi and I became much better acquainted and I finally got up enough nerve to ask her if she wanted to go for a stroll with me the next day and to my surprise and great joy she said, *"I would love to."* I thought my heart would jump out of my chest. It was all I could do to keep her from seeing how excited I was. Now I have to wait forever for the next day to arrive.

When I got home, I had a snack, hoping that I could get to sleep right away so that the night would pass quickly. The night had a mind of its own and I stayed awake half the night thinking about what I would do to impress Fifi.

I must have worried myself to sleep because all of a sudden it was morning.

THOMAS

10

ZIPPER'S DATE

"*Oh boy, it's morning,*" I said as I sprang up to prepare myself for the day. Today is the day that I get to take Fifi for a walk around in my world. I must make a good impression, so I have to look my best and be on my best behavior.

I will surely introduce her to all my friends and take her to all our favorite places to play. I'll have to teach her to walk the high wire without fear of falling so that she will have a safe refuge in emergencies.

Well, I'm all set to meet Fifi, so I'm off to her house. When I arrived, I found Harry asleep in the corner as usual and Clancy was busy shelling nuts for lunch. Then I saw Fifi, boy, was she pretty! "*Uh, Hi,*" I said, trying my best not to get my words all tangled up. "*Are you ready to go for a walk today?*" Fifi replied, "*I certainly am, I have waited all day for our walk, I'm so excited.*" That was all I needed to hear as I took her by the hand and outside we went.

She asked,"*Where are we going first?*" I said, "*I want to show you where Clancy and I go to find all the nuts that we store up for winter.*" With that we were off to see the big Oak trees and Pecan trees that we loved so well.

While we were searching for Howard, we ran into Skippy who was happy to meet Fifi. He said, "*I'm happy to meet you, I've heard so much about you from Zipper.*" Fifi said,"*Oh, really. Does he talk about me?*" Skippy said "*All the time*"

All the attention was making Fifi glow and was making me red in the face. I wanted her to know that I thought of her all the time, so I didn't mind too much. I told Skippy we were trying to find Howard so that he could meet her and he said, *"I saw him this morning, but not in the last few hours. I'll help you look for him."*

Ever so often we stopped to rest under a tree and when we sat down, Fifi would look over at me and I would just melt. *"She really likes me"*, I thought as I smiled back at her. After a short rest we continued to search for Howard, but were unable to find him.

We enjoyed the afternoon playing at the new house construction that was going on until it was starting to get a little dark. It was time to go home now and we said good-by to Skippy and returned home.

I said to Fifi,*"I certainly hope you had a good day and I wish we could do it again, if it's alright with you."* Fifi said, *"Yes, I had a wonderful day and yes, we can do it again, soon I hope."* That was the answer I had hoped for so I said,*"We will do it again, soon!"*

11

ZIPPER GETS A SHOCK

Fifi and I had several weeks of being together enjoying nature and getting to know each other better. One evening when we returned, we were sitting together looking through her door when all of a sudden, out of the clear blue sky, she leaned over and kissed me on the cheek. That was totally unexpected and shocked me so bad that I couldn't speak.

She must have thought I was nuts because I didn't know what to say or do. I had never been kissed before and I was simply stunned. I had wanted this to happen one day, but I wasn't expecting it when it finally happened. After a few moments I turned and looked at her. She was radiant with her big eyes looking straight at me with a warm smile on her face. There was no need to speak, we both understood what was happening. We were in love!

When I finally came back to Earth I said to her, "*Fifi, I'm in love with you!*" Surprisingly, she answered, "*I love you too Zipper.*" Then I put my arms around her and held her ever so tenderly for a long while.

After that day we became even closer and enjoyed every minute that we shared together. Sometimes she would come over to my house and help me clean the place up. I convinced Woody to make a new window for me on the backside of the tree big enough for Fifi and myself to sit and look over the neighborhood.

We spent many evenings sitting by the window, hugging and kissing each other. We were so happy, but we both knew that something was missing and we knew what it was.

One evening when we were by the window, the evening sun was coming in warming both of us, and it felt good.

Zipper and Friends

I turned to Fifi and said, *"Fifi, would you like to get married?"* Her eyes got even bigger than usual and a great big smile came on her face as she said, *"Yes, I would love to be your wife Zipper."*

Now that the decision was made we both felt much better and started thinking about setting a date and inviting everyone to attend. There were a lot of plans to be made and we wasted no time in getting the details worked out.

Fifi said, *"We can ask Hootie, the village Elder to do the ceremony and have a nice reception in the park just a block away. We will let your house become our home, naturally I would have to add the female touch to it. He had no curtains over the window and no lacy things here and there, but that was easy to fix."*

We both were eager to get the deed done, so we set the date for the next month on Harry's birthday.

39

12

THE WEDDING PLANS

As Fifi and I started planning the big event, we decided to ask everyone to attend that wanted to including the meanies, Thomas and Henry. I said to Fifi, *"Do you think it's wise to invite them? They are our worst enemies."* She said, *"We can invite them, whether they come or not is their choice."* I said, *"Well, I had better get busy searching for everyone to ask them to come."*

Angie was busy caring for her new babies, with Woodys help and they were very excited upon hearing the news. Angie asked, *"Is it ok if I bring my babies along?"* I said, *"Of course it's ok, Bring anyone you like."*

Fifi will ask Harry and Clancy, so it's up to me to invite Henry, Thomas, Howard, Skippy, and anyone else I run into. I found Skippy playing with his ball in the road. I yelled, *"Skippy!, What are you doing playing in the road? Aren't you afraid you may be struck by a car?"* He replied, *"I was having so much fun, I didn't think and wound up on the road. Thank you for stopping me."*

I said, *"I would play with you for a while, but I have an important mission today and I don't have any spare time."* I explained to Skippy that Fifi and I were planning to get married and we would like him to attend the event. Skippy said, *"You mean you are getting married and won't be able to play with your friends anymore?"* I said, *"No Skippy, that's not what it means at all. It means that it's time for me to get married and think about having a family of my own, maybe even some little ones. Then as they get old enough, we all could do things together."* Skippy said, *"Gee,* that sounds great, sure I'll come. Now I have to think of a gift for you two. Now I'm all excited."

I said to Skippy,"Why don't you come along with me and we can find Howard. We can also ask everyone else we meet if they would like to come." Skippy said, "Ok, we might make some new friends along the way, that would be great." And with that they were off.

When they found Howard he was playing in the creek behind the Bensons house. He was having a good time finding crawfish in the creek. They were ugly things and didn't do a thing for my appetite, but to him they were very tasty. I said to him, "Guess what? Fifi and I are getting married!" He said, "Well, that's no surprise, I was wondering when you would come to that decision. I knew you two were getting closer with every passing day." I said, "We would like you to come and bring anyone else you can find because we are having the ceremony in the park with a party afterwards", he answered, *"Sure, I'll come and I know a couple of others that would like to come also."*

Now all that was left was to invite Henry and Thomas. That would have to be done with great care. It would be nice to have them as friends, but I am so afraid of them. I know what I'll do. I'll go up on the power lines, high above and ask them, that way they can't get me. I finally found them and yelled down asking them if they would like to come. Henry said, *"You mean you want us to come and celebrate with you, aren't you afraid?"* I replied, *"Yes, but can't you be friendly to us just this once, it means a lot to Fifi to have everyone there."* Thomas said, *"Well, maybe we can come if you really want us to. This is not some kind of trick is it?"* I said, *"Heavens no! We would be happy if you came."* With that my task was finished. Now all I had to do was figure out how to get some treats for the party that everyone would like.

13

WEDDING DAY

At long last, the big day has arrived. It looks like everyone we invited is here, even some that I had never met. This was great. We always cherish meeting new friends. It was a beautiful day with good warm sunshine coming down and there was not a cloud in the sky. Even Henry and Thomas were here. I have often wondered why they never chased each other. I always thought cats and dogs were enemies.

I didn't know much about the village Elder that was to perform the ceremony. He was an Owl, rumored to be very wise and honorable. His name was "Hootie", I guess because he was always saying, "Who".

Now it was time for everything to start. When Fifi appeared, you could have toppled me over with a feather. She was so beautiful and seemed to glow with excitement. Everyone was saying "Ooh" and how radiant she looked. I have to say, I was fairly handsome myself, all primped up for the occasion.

Hootie yelled out, *"Everyone take your positions please, so we can get started."* Once we were all set to go Hootie said, *"Let's all bow our heads and ask the Lord for his blessings on this couple."* We all bowed our heads and as I glanced around even Henry and Thomas were doing the same. I was glad that things were going so well.

After Hootie finished the prayer, he began the ceremony. I didn't hear a lot of what he said. It felt like I was deaf about half the time. I was shaking like a leaf. I was holding her hand so tight and shaking so much that Fifi let out a little giggle right in the middle of the ceremony and Hootie said, *"Is something wrong, are you sure you want* to go on?" I replied, "Oh yes", we're just so happy." With that, the next thing I heard was Hootie saying, "I now pronounce you husband and wife." Upon hearing that, and with tears in our eyes we kissed each other to seal the deal.

Everyone was cheering and clapping as Hootie said, "It is now my pleasure to present to you our newest happy couple, Zipper and Fifi."

With that, Harry sprang up and said, "Just a minute, you can't claim to be married until you do the traditional feat of jumping the broom handle!" He promptly produced a broom and with Harry and Clancy holding either end, we jumped over it together. After everyone took their turn kissing the bride, we were off to the park to celebrate.

As everyone started to eat and drink Henry and Thomas came over and congratulated us. They seemed nice enough so I asked them, "Why have you not tried to catch us like you usually do?" Henry said, "Catch you? We never wanted to do that. You think that all the rumors you have heard are true, but that's all they are, rumors!" I said, "Then why are you always chasing us and scaring us half to death?" Thomas answered, "We never wanted to hurt you. All we wanted was to play and that's the only way we knew how. Honestly, I don't know what we would have done when we finally caught you. We just wanted to be friends in our own way!"

I said, "Wow", that's wonderful to hear. We have always been terrified of you because of the rumors." Henry said, "I know, people should never spread rumors. There is no telling how many problems have been caused by rumors."

Now that we understand, we can play together often. I said, "Come Henry, let me fix you a plate of goodies". Fifi did the same for Thomas and we were so happy that all has worked out so well.

All of our friends and guests were having a great time getting to know each other and it was starting to get late in the day. Everyone began to go their own way feeling happy for a wonderful day's events.

Fifi and I arrived at my, *oops*, our house and I scooped her up and carried her through the door. To say we were happy doesn't come close to our true feelings. We had made many new friends, even those we thought were our enemies and now it was the beginning of a new life for both of us. We were soul mates now, sure to live happily ever after.

THE END

www.ingramcontent.com/pod-product-compliance
Lightning Source LLC
Chambersburg PA
CBHW081723270326
41933CB00017B/3281

9 780692 447451